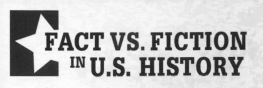
FACT VS. FICTION
IN U.S. HISTORY

THE FIRST
THANKSGIVING

SEPARATING FACT FROM FICTION

by Peter Mavrikis

Consultant: Katrina Phillips, PhD

CAPSTONE PRESS
a capstone imprint

Capstone Captivate is published by Capstone Press, an imprint of Capstone.
1710 Roe Crest Drive
North Mankato, Minnesota 56003
capstonepub.com

Library of Congress Cataloging-in-Publication Data
Names: Mavrikis, Peter, author.
Title: The first Thanksgiving : separating fact from fiction / by Peter Mavrikis.
Description: North Mankato, Minnesota : Capstone Press, a Capstone imprint, [2022] | Series: Fact vs. fiction in U.S. history | Includes bibliographical references and index. | Audience: Ages 8-11 | Audience: Grades 4-6 | Summary: "Every November, the United States celebrates Thanksgiving Day. But what actually happened at the first Thanksgiving? And when did it happen? Discover the facts and find out the fiction surrounding one of America's favorite holidays"— Provided by publisher.
Identifiers: LCCN 2021002512 | ISBN 9781496695666 (hardcover) | ISBN 9781496696762 (paperback) | ISBN 9781977155023 (pdf) | ISBN 9781977156648 (kindle edition)
Subjects: LCSH: Massachusetts—History—New Plymouth, 1620-1691—Juvenile literature. | Pilgrims (New Plymouth Colony)—Juvenile literature. | Wampanoag Indians—Juvenile literature. | Thanksgiving Day—History—Juvenile literature. | United States—History—Errors, inventions, etc.—Juvenile literature.
Classification: LCC F68 .M435 2022 | DDC 974.4/02—dc23
LC record available at https://lccn.loc.gov/2021002512

Image Credits
Associated Press: Jim Cole, 27, Julia Cumes, 17, The Hazleton Standard-Speaker/Warren Ruda, 5; Bridgeman Images: Peter Newark Pictures, 15; Dreamstime: Steven Cukrov, 28; Getty Images: ivan-96, 24, The Boston Globe/Pam Berry, 20, whitemay, 6, ZU_09, cover (top right), 25; Library of Congress: cover (top left), 9, 10, 12; Mary Evans Picture Library: 16; Newscom: AiWire, 18, ZUMA Press/Charles Mahaux, 23; North Wind Picture Archives: cover (bottom), 11, 13, 14, 22; Shutterstock: JeniFoto, back cover, 21; XNR Productions: 8

Editorial Credits
Editor: Gena Chester; Designer: Tracy Davies; Media Researcher: Svetlana Zhurkin; Production Specialist: Laura Manthe

Thank you to our consultant, Katrina Phillips, PhD, enrolled member of the Red Cliff Band of Lake Superior Ojibwe

All internet sites appearing in back matter were available and accurate when this book was sent to press.

Table of Contents

Words in **bold** are in the glossary.

Introduction

Each year in November, many schools across the United States perform plays about the first Thanksgiving. The Pilgrims are often shown wearing black and white clothing. The Native Americans may have feathers tucked in their hair—an untrue representation that dates back to paintings by white artists from the early 1900s. Some classroom productions may even have a papier-mâché version of Plymouth Rock.

A meal celebrating a harvest and cooperation happened 400 years ago, in 1621. That's a fact. But what parts of the story are untrue, or fiction? What really happened? Were the Pilgrims forced to leave England in search of religious freedom? Were the Pilgrims and the Native Americans they encountered—the Wampanoag Nation—friends? And was turkey even on the menu? Let's begin separating fact from fiction.

Schoolchildren across the country perform traditional Thanksgiving programs each year, but how accurate are they?

Chapter 1

Seeking Religious Freedom

In the 1600s, England was ruled by King James I. He believed that all people under his rule should join the Church of England. Some people from England did not agree. They called themselves Separatists or Puritans. King James sent those who did not follow his rules to jail for their religious beliefs. By 1608, many Puritans fled to Holland to escape religious **persecution**.

A group of Puritan men attend a prayer meeting.

A New World?

Thousands of miles west of England, European adventurers were exploring the lands west of the European continent, now called North and South America. Many European countries, including England, saw this land as an opportunity to gain wealth and expand their rule. Many European people referred to this land as the New World.

But this is fiction. The land was not new. It had been home to many **Indigenous** or Native American groups for thousands of years before the first Europeans ever set foot there. These groups were organized into Nations and other larger communities. Each Nation had their own language, culture, customs, and beliefs, and still do today.

A New Life

In Holland, the Puritans were allowed to worship freely without fear of being punished. But good-paying jobs were hard to find. The Puritans were also worried that their children were becoming more **Dutch** than English. After 12 years in Holland, the Puritans decided to make their next move. This time, they would travel across the Atlantic Ocean to the place they called the "New World." There they would start a new community that would allow them to practice their religion. The Puritans also hoped to make a good living and **profit** from the **resources** and land they had heard about.

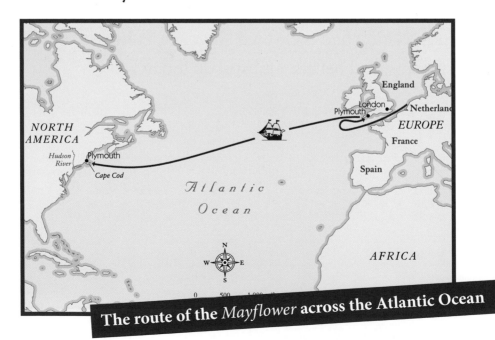

The route of the *Mayflower* **across the Atlantic Ocean**

On September 6, 1620, the *Mayflower* set sail from Southampton, England. The 102 Puritans onboard were looking forward to a new life.

Fact!

The word Pilgrim wasn't used until the 1800s. Before then, many Americans called this first wave of Puritans "first-comers" or "forefathers."

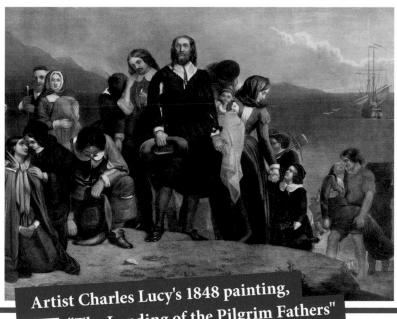

Artist Charles Lucy's 1848 painting, "The Landing of the Pilgrim Fathers"

Chapter 2

Plymouth Rock

It was nearly fall when the *Mayflower* left England. After a month of smooth sailing, the weather turned rough. The Pilgrims spent most of the journey crammed below deck. Many were seasick. There wasn't enough food or water. Finally, after more than two months at sea, land was spotted on November 9, 1620. Two days later, they landed at what is now known as Plymouth Rock.

Fact!

It was planned that two ships would set sail from England—the *Speedwell* and the *Mayflower*. However, the *Speedwell* was unable to make the journey due to leaks, leaving the *Mayflower* to sail alone.

Destination: New York

The *Mayflower* set its original course for what is now New York. At the time, New York was a region of what the Europeans called Northern Virginia. The Pilgrims planned on settling along the Hudson River. But the weather on their journey turned rough, and the ship went off course. When the Pilgrims landed, they were 220 miles (354 kilometers) north of New York, in what is now Massachusetts.

Native Americans lived in villages all along the eastern coast, such as Pomelock (above), near present-day North Carolina. Wherever the Pilgrims had landed, they would have been on Native American lands.

Landfall

The story goes that the Pilgrims landed in Cape Cod Bay on a granite rock later named Plymouth Rock. However, there is no proof that this was the exact location of their arrival.

Due to bad weather, the *Mayflower* was forced to take shelter from the rough seas in the natural harbor of present-day Provincetown, Massachusetts. When they were able to disembark the *Mayflower* and begin building the settlement, the **colonizers** signed the Mayflower Compact. This document, now lost to history, set the rules the Pilgrims agreed to follow in the **colony** they would establish.

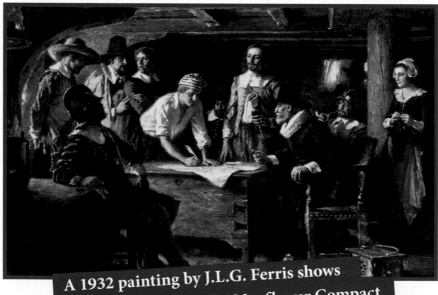

A 1932 painting by J.L.G. Ferris shows Pilgrims signing the Mayflower Compact.

The Great Dying

When the Pilgrims stepped onto the beach of Cape Cod, they found a deserted village, empty fields, and discarded tools. But they found none of the Indigenous people who had once lived there. A disease brought by European traders and sailors several years earlier had devastated the village. Between 1616 and 1619, many thousands of Indigenous people—as much as 90 percent of the coastal population—may have perished. The Wampanoag Nation call this time the "Great Dying."

Woodcut art depicts the tragic losses of the Wampanoag people from smallpox and other diseases brought by Europeans.

Chapter 3

The First Thanksgiving?

Winter was quickly approaching when the *Mayflower* landed. The Pilgrims needed to find a place to build homes. They explored the area and found a spot near a brook. It showed evidence of the Great Dying: plowed fields, empty homes, and storehouses of supplies, which the Pilgrims took. They named it New Plymouth, after a town in England.

The first winter in New Plymouth was difficult. The colonizers were running low on food, and it was too late for planting. More than half of them died from hunger and disease. Called the "Starving Time," things looked bad for the Pilgrims.

Pilgrims built New Plymouth on land that had once held a Wampanoag village.

By March 1621, the Wampanoag Nation's grand sachem or chief, Massasoit, and his translator, a Patuxet man named Tisquantum, met the Pilgrims. The Wampanoag people taught the Pilgrims how to plant crops, farm, and hunt in the region. Six months later, the Pilgrims celebrated their first successful harvest.

SQUANTO

Tisquantum, also known as Squanto, was from the Patuxet band of the Wampanoag Nation. He was one of the Native people who taught the Pilgrims how to live off the land. He was also one of the few Native people who spoke the English language. Back in 1614, Tisquantum had been kidnapped by a group of English explorers and taken to England. He learned English during his enslavement. Tisquantum returned to Massachusetts in 1618 only to find that his village had been deserted. The Patuxet people had died of diseases brought by the Europeans. Only a few years later, the Pilgrims picked the same location to colonize.

Tisquantum taught the Pilgrims survival skills for the region.

Harvest Celebrations

The feast observed by the Pilgrims and Native Americans was not the first celebration of its kind. Communities around the world had celebrated successful harvests for many centuries. Ancient cultures, including the Egyptians, Greeks, and Romans, held special celebrations after a good growing season. They gave thanks to their gods and goddesses. The Pilgrims celebrated Harvest Home in England—a day spent singing hymns, praying, and sharing baskets of food.

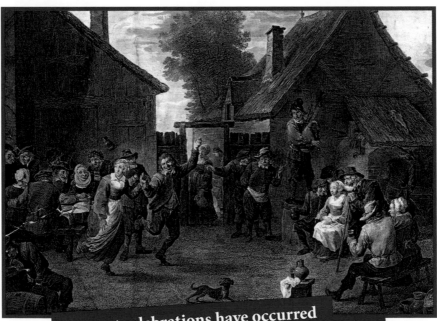

Harvest celebrations have occurred throughout history and across cultures.

In North America, Indigenous communities honored the harvest with celebrations such as Harvest Moon, Green Corn, or Fruit Moon. The events included eating, dancing, and giving thanks.

Fact!

The Wampanoag are known as the "People of the First Light." They are the original inhabitants of what is now southeastern Massachusetts and eastern Rhode Island. Today, most Wampanoag people live on reservations in Massachusetts.

In 2007, members of the Wampanoag Nation celebrated the official recognition of their tribe by the U.S. government.

Chapter 4

Please Pass the Turkey

The Pilgrims' harvest was **bountiful**. Thanks to the Wampanoag, the Pilgrims were able to grow beans, corns, and squash. Now it was time for the Pilgrims to give thanks and celebrate.

"The First Thanksgiving at Plymouth" by Jennie Augusta Brownscombe (1914) is a popular portrayal of the event in 1621. However, the painting shows many things that are not true to history.

Many stories of the Pilgrims' celebration center around a painting by an American artist named Jennie Augusta Brownscombe (1850–1936). It is perhaps the most famous painting of the event referred to as the first Thanksgiving. However, like most other paintings of the event, Brownscombe's portrayal is not accurate.

"The First Thanksgiving at Plymouth," painted in 1914, shows Pilgrims and Wampanoag sharing food on a long table covered by white linen. The Pilgrims are dressed in their finest clothing. Wampanoag are shown with feathers in their hair. The scene in the painting does not show what happened or what the Pilgrims and Native Americans actually ate. The clothing pictured is not correct. The Wampanoag are shown in clothing that was commonly worn by Native Americans living 2,000 miles (3,200 km) away in the Midwestern region of the United States, such as headdresses of the Great Sioux Nation.

What's on the Menu?

Today's traditional Thanksgiving meal includes foods like roasted turkey, stuffing, corn, mashed potatoes, gravy, green beans, and cranberry sauce. For dessert, perhaps a pumpkin or pecan pie. The meal at New Plymouth consisted of roasted deer, geese, and ducks. Seafood, including cod, clams, and even eel, was part of the meal. The vegetables served were corn, squash, peas, beans, and pumpkin.

An actor shows how a goose would have been cooked in New Plymouth.

THE CORNUCOPIA

For many Americans, the Thanksgiving holiday brings to mind the image of the cornucopia. The cornucopia is a woven basket filled with the vegetables and fruits that we imagine were eaten during early Thanksgivings. The truth is the cornucopia has been around for thousands of years. The word "cornucopia" comes from Latin and is a combination of the words *cornu* (horn) and *copia* (plenty). It is an ancient symbol of abundance and a popular decoration placed on dinner tables during Thanksgiving.

Fact!

At one time, the Founders considered making the turkey the national bird of the United States. In 1782, they decided to go with the bald eagle instead.

A Three-Day Feast

Many stories about the first Thanksgiving center on the Pilgrims and the Wampanoag sharing a meal together. But there is no evidence that an invitation was sent to the Wampanoag. Instead, Wampanoag people may have been drawn to the area to investigate the sounds of **musket** fire as the Pilgrims hunted ducks and wild birds. Chief Massasoit and other Wampanoag men joined the hunt, adding deer to the menu. For three days, the Pilgrims and the Wampanoag ate, played, relaxed, and ate some more.

An artist depicted Wampanoag offering a deer to the Pilgrims.

Although it was a time for celebration, the Pilgrims did not wear fancy clothing. They also did not wear tall black hats with shiny buckles, as Thanksgiving decorations of today suggest. Instead, the Pilgrims dressed plainly. The men wore floppy hats, long-sleeved shirts, and pants. They wore

An actor from a living history museum portrays a Native American woman from the 1600s tending a fire.

close-fitting jackets called doublets, unless it was too warm. The women wore simple waistcoats and aprons.

We also know that the Wampanoag did not wear feathered headdresses as shown in Brownscombe's inaccurate painting. This portrayal is fiction. Wampanoag men and women wore leggings and moccasins. The woman also wore skirts with fringes.

Chapter 5

Tension Builds

The 1621 feast was more than just a celebration for a good harvest. It observed the **alliance** between the Wampanoag and the Pilgrims. If one side needed help, like the Pilgrims did during their first winter in New Plymouth, the other side would assist.

At the time, the Wampanoag Nation was fighting with the Narragansett Nation. Because of the European diseases that had killed many Wampanoag, their side was outnumbered. The Wampanoag offered their help to the Pilgrims in exchange for weapons to aid in their fight with the Narragansett.

Chief Massasoit was committed to peace with the Pilgrims.

The End of Peace

But peace between the two groups did not last. As more Europeans arrived, hostilities grew. Many of the Europeans were **racist** toward Native Americans. The Pilgrims believed the land now belonged to them. By 1630, thousands of colonizers lived in the area. They forced the Native Americans out of their homelands.

KING PHILIP'S WAR (1675–1678)

In 1675, the Wampanoag and the English colonizers were at war. Chief Massasoit's son, Metacom, was the Wampanoag sachem during this time. Metacom originally worked with the colonizers and even took the English name of Philip and the title "King" in place of Chief. After years of giving up property, including land and **ammunition**, King Philip wanted to stop the English from taking control of Indigenous lands. The Wampanoag, together with other Native American Nations in the region, attacked English settlements across the

Massachusetts Bay Colony. The English responded by attacking many Indigenous villages that supported King Philip's War. The war ended when King Philip was killed. Thousands died on both sides. Many settlements and villages were destroyed.

Chapter 6

Making It Official

Some people believe that Thanksgiving has been celebrated every year since the 1621 feast the Wampanoag and Pilgrims shared. That is far from true.

Nearly everything we know about the original event comes from William Bradford. He was leader of New Plymouth and served as its governor for 30 years. He is also famous for keeping a journal called "Of Plimoth Plantation." His records of Plymouth Colony and the Pilgrims provides much of what we know about them.

Bradford and Chief Massasoit worked hard to keep the peace between European colonizers and Wampanoag. But new leaders took over, and it became more difficult to avoid conflict. For the next 200 years, a harvest celebration between any of the Native American Nations and European colonizers was likely never repeated.

A National Holiday

In 1837, a magazine editor named Sarah Hale tried to convince U.S. President Zachary Taylor to create a national holiday called Thanksgiving. At the time, Thanksgiving was celebrated by some families in the northeast region of the United States. Hale wanted all Americans to celebrate it. She hoped it would bring people from across the country together and create an American tradition. But her efforts did not succeed with President Taylor. She also failed with Presidents Millard Fillmore, Franklin Pierce, and James Buchanan. It took almost 30 years before Hale's luck changed.

Sarah Hale

During the Civil War (1861–1865), Hale reached out to President Abraham Lincoln. Lincoln had been looking for a way to create unity among the states. In 1863, thanks to the efforts of Sarah Hale, Lincoln declared Thanksgiving a national holiday. In 1941, Congress made it official. Thanksgiving became a national holiday to be celebrated on the fourth Thursday of each November.

Thanksgiving does not have the same meaning for everyone, though. Many Americans love the holiday and time spent with family giving thanks. But for other Americans, Thanksgiving is also a reminder of the painful history created by the arrival of European colonizers. For many Native American people, colonization resulted in displacement from their homes, war, disease, and death. Thanksgiving is a day to remember this history and honor the first people of the nation.

A National Day of Mourning sign in Plymouth, Massachusetts, recognizes the losses Native Americans experienced when Europeans came to their land.

Timeline

1603–1625	King James I rules England
1608	Many Puritans leave England to avoid religious persecution
1616–1619	The "Great Dying," a time when millions of Native Americans died from diseases brought by Europeans
September 6, 1620	The *Mayflower* sets sail from Southampton, England
November 9, 1620	The Pilgrims reach the coast of present-day Massachusetts
November 11, 1620	The Mayflower Compact is signed
December 1620	The settlers begin building Plymouth Colony (New Plymouth)
March 1621	The Wampanoag teach the Pilgrims how to plant and hunt
September–November 1621	The Pilgrims and Wampanoag celebrate what is often referred to as the "first" Thanksgiving
1630	Thousands of colonizers settle in New England
1675–1678	King Philip's War
1837	Magazine editor Sarah Hale proposes making Thanksgiving a holiday
1863	President Abraham Lincoln declares Thanksgiving a national holiday
1941	Congress passes a law making Thanksgiving a national holiday

Glossary

alliance (ah-LIE-unss)—when two or more different groups agree to help each other and work together

ammunition (am-yoo-NIH-shun)—bullets and other objects that can be fired from weapons

bountiful (BOWN-tih-ful)—a large amount or supply

colonizer (KAH-luh-nye-zer)—a person who settles an area and takes control of it in the name of their home country

colony (KAH-luh-nee)—a settlement under the control of the home country

Dutch (DUTCH)—relating to the Netherlands (Holland)

Indigenous (in-DIH-jen-us)—native or belonging to an area; Native American people are indigenous to the Americas

musket (MUSS-ket)—a type of long gun

persecution (per-suh-KYOO-shun)—to treat a person or group cruelly because they believe differently

profit (PRAH-fit)—the money made after all costs are paid

racist (RAY-sist)—being prejudiced against a person or group of a different race based on negative beliefs

resource (REE-sorss)—something that has value and use

Read More

Byers, Ann. *Squanto*. New York: Cavendish Square Publishing, LLC, 2021.

Woodland, Faith. *Thanksgiving*. New York: Smartbook Media Inc., 2021.

Yomtov, Nel. *Plymouth Rock*. North Mankato, MN: Capstone, 2021.

Internet Sites

The History Channel: Thanksgiving
history.com/topics/thanksgiving/history-of-thanksgiving

Mayflower History
mayflowerhistory.com/pilgrim-history/

Plimoth Plantation
plimoth.org/

Index